ALSO B

Audio Recordings

Theresa tha Songbird Speaks (2007)

Transmission (2009)

B.I.R.D. Is The Word (2012)

Chi-Town Hustle (2013)

Sunset in B.I.R.D.Land (2015)

1

MASS MATTER MAGIC

Be Great
Be Light
Be Love
Theresa the
Skylind

4

By THERESA M. WILSON

B.I.R.D. Media Enterprises, LLC
2016

First Printing: 2017
ISBN-13: 978-1542914215
B.I.R.D. Media Enterprises, LLC
19 Ollie St NW
Atlanta, GA 30314
thasongbird.wix.com/thasongbird

Interior Photography Credit: Phyllis Iller/ Melissa Alexander

Cover Photography Credit: ClickArtist Media/ Maurice Thompson

For the women.
For the writing,
breathing,
fighting,
healing,
overcoming,
supernatural
women.

CONTENTS

MAGIC

ACKNOWLEDGMENTS

To Mom and Dad- you are awesome sources of God's love. Thank you for making me a product of that love.

To Meke & Tam, and all my universal sisters- you make everything better! Always. Thank you for keeping me sane, calling me on my shit and pushing me towards my goals.

I couldn't begin to list all the artists I want to thank who inspire me. In a world succumb with turmoil you give me hope for the future of art and humanity.

Thank you to my family EVERYWHERE.

To all my ancestors- Thank you for the drops and ripples that have turned into waves to carry me.

To Maurice, Terry, Sa'alek and Melissa. Eternal friends and my personal millionaire posse. I LOVE you guys.

To Pages Matam and my editing and proof readers- your feedback was monumental and this book could not have happened without you.

To T-Laine, I can't wait to be a book (collection) in your library, I love you SO much!

To my wonderful philanthropic family:
Chidinma Asonye, A. D. Carson, Nicole Young, Sarajini Nunn, Shetee Williams, Carol Payne, Jillian Frank, Sheneka Peterson, Antwan Thorbs, Karena Butler, Gonza Kaijage, Toni Brown, Lydia Ellis, Jan Hobbs, George Mass, Lauren Eldridge, Tameka Wonsley-Gilkey, and The Garrett Family

And I would like to especially thank you, for reading.

To The Reader

MASS:

1) the property of matter that determines the force required to impart acceleration to an object
2) the majority of
3) as relating to/affecting large numbers of people
4) assemble or cause to assemble into one body

MATTER:

1) a physical substance, distinct from mind and spirit
2) a topic
3) being of importance
4) of a wound

MAGIC:
1) the power to influence events using mysterious or supernatural powers
2) having supernatural powers
3) wonderful; exciting
4) move, change or create as if supernatural

This book serves as a reminder that at the beginning middle and end of it all:

I am MASS
I am MATTER
I am MAGIC

MASS

MATTER

MAGIC

The Punchline

It's funny
Most times
You don't know you're doing something difficult
Until it gets difficult to do
Or until you watch someone struggle with a skill
That you have already mastered

It's funny
Strength has value
But you become strong
By finding out where you are weak
Why you are insecure
Strength is not a cure
It's a Band-Aid
To help you ignore the sore spots
Endure the pain
Colliding with the soft tissue is unavoidable
Growing stronger brings all of one's vulnerabilities
To light

It's funny
When I stopped fucking these brothers
They managed
To keep fucking with me

It's funny
You can give away your power
Even if you don't give away your pussy
You don't have to open your legs

To open your heart
You can still be so lonely
With someone there beside you

It's funny
I have spent my day in and out of tears
Not wanting to disappear
Not wanting to be held
Touched
Fucked
Loved
Just
Needing to talk
Needing to listen

It's funny
How folks you don't know
Speak to your soul
Strangers
Often give the best advice
And once it's utilized
You realized they might have saved your life
And you never get to tell them
Thank you

It's funny

So This is Life

Mine has been convoluted and complicated
You think it's so long until someone close to you is gone
Striving with all your might to be right
When you know you're dead ass wrong
Mustering a smile to stay bright when inside you feel so numb

Is this my life?

The love and the like
The could and the might
Got me crying alone in the middle of the night
Searching for an inner light
With a doubt I'll ever find a way out
Somedays I'm just trying to survive it
Somedays on auto pilot
Some days on cruise control
No maps
No way back
No take backs
No Indian giving
No level playing fields
To keep in real
Having hoop dreams don't guarantee
I'll make the squad
No guarantees I will ever touch the ball
Everybody's arms aren't long enough to reach the stars
Seems like God made all of the decisions hard
From the start

I've made mistakes
Made as many moves as I could make
Put all my eggs in one place singing
The roof
The roof
The roof is on fire
We don't need no water
Let the motherfucker burn
Learned to
Take turns
Take what I earn
Take what I deserve
Take these suckers for everything that they're worth
But know which master to serve
So who's the master, Leroy?
So fast to destroy the God in man
Then recreate him,
Her,
It
All over again
Reclaim it
Like language
Like lineage
Like his, hers, ours, mine
MINE
Hours mine themselves into memories and become time
Time become a noose
And time stays tugging on that line
Snatching breaths with every step until the inventory declines
Until there's nothing left on the shelf
But there's still people in line

Defined by our names
Places of origin
Birthdays, astrological signs
Religions and next of kin
The quality of our homes and friends
Social security numbers, taxes brackets and break ups
Hiccups
Bicycles
Skinned knees
Painful memories
Resilience
Brilliance
Salt wrapped in chocolate
Bittersweet at the finish
Finite and never ending
Extra sensory and senseless
Boxes of band aids
And relationships that can't be mended
People I will never forget

Regret
This nagging need for respect
Everything in between the first blink and death
My phoned in mediocre efforts
My worst and my best

Maybe not in that order
But there is no such thing as order
In this place made of chaos
Beautifully orchestrated chaos
Holding miracles in the most unsuspecting places

More often taken for granted
More often more than my mortal mind can manage
Life still
And always will
Continues to amaze
With grace that calls itself coincidence
And coincidentally today
Is one of the better ones
Could be the best one I've ever done
Once the clutter is cleared away

Used To

Early morning
No Wi-Fi connection
So no laptop
No emails
No social media
Just me
Last night's leftover trees
The words and feelings I've been avoiding
A few games on my tablet
To provide a distraction
Too early
Too quiet
Nothing is happening
I'm trying to find the noise
Make the noise
Be the noisiest
Squeakiest wheel
For the attention that it yields
Trying to make my mind work right
Provide myself some insight
Despite how it used to be
Trying not to miss how it used to be
Because truthfully
I used to be homeless
Helpless
Reckless
Distracted
I used to have lack
No self-restraint

I used to think I was a saint
Even when I knew I was a sinner
I used to think I wasn't shit
Even though I've always been a winner
I still think of what I left outside
When I'm focused on my center
I can't help but to remember
I can't help but to notice the embers
And remember how they used to glow
Used to
But it don't no more

William's Women

I'm a daddy's girl
Little does he know
Much does he see
Never tells me
But he prays quietly
That my life won't battle me
The way he battled his
Little does he know
If I had half of his endurance and his will
His ability to survive, provide, and protect
Then I would always be able to take care of myself

I know the man who sits on the couch
Only goes out
To fish
Work
Go to church
Golf
And tend his garden
I grew up thinking life had hardened him
Somehow

He never gets loud

Only shouts to call us down to eat

He prays, plans, speaks

Quietly

My daddy don't play

Not easily impressed or swayed

He doesn't drink

Curse

Smoke

Alpha male

Straight laced

With traces of history he never shares

The man he was before we were there

The women

The wife and the children

Old pictured of him reveal

What my mother finds so appealing

The boy she knew at 19

Army enlisted

Vietnam missions

The specialized marksmen's vision

Now relegated to a golfer's precision

The man from Madison county

Tact with horses and card counting
Came from nothing much but always made enough
Turns dirt and seeds into bounty
I will never know the alcoholic addict
Controlled by his habit
Who could always spot if I had been
Doing anything more than
Smoking a little weed
I will never see
The prototypes
And obsolete versions of
Man he used to be

His history is no secret
The battles he's defeated go unseen
He doesn't share them as life lessons to his offspring
He allows his living to be proof
Of what God and hard work can do
His family is the testimony of a lowly sinner
Mama hugs us
Dad prepares the dinner
Buys the Christmas gifts in the winter
The gifts he's given me
Have been essential to my symmetry

Every bit of my grit and low tolerance for bullshit

Tenacious work ethic

Solid when the world gets hectic

Quietly protective

Sometimes I neglect to acknowledge how much light

He provides to my brilliance

He gave me my name

When he hears it

It fills him

With love

With pride

With honor for his wife

With honor for the sacrifices he's made for his daughters

So I sing for my father

For him having the heart to

Because it's hard to be a man

And make the difficult decisions

To fall into submission

To the will of the women

In your life

To the God who made it right

When he'd done it wrong for so long

He finds the strength to go on

Wise beyond wealth

Silent and stealth

Dangerous and elegant

Country, hard and delicate

A hell of a man

Steadfast

My dad

Hiccups

Necessary nuisance
Bobbles in your path
Pebbles in your shoes
Gaps of air in your breathing tubes
Jerking at the center of your being
The abrasive friend you always appreciate leaving
Because they don't stay very long

Toughen the lungs
Strengthen the diaphragm
Tenacious and stifling
Force you to focus on how you speak and how you act
Bring you back to reality
When you thought you had everything
These next few moments take all of your concentration
The unsuspecting spaces in the making of the places
Where you know it's supposed to flow

Forced to grow the hell up
Faster than you expected
Sooner than you desired
Reminder of how you've neglected
Your small eternal fire
So quickly snuffed out and re-ignited
Snuffed out and then it's like
It never even happened

Somehow you're still in tact
In fact, you're a little bit taller
Walking with a longer stride
A bit more fire in your eyes
Gratitude in your attitude
God's grabbing you
And snapping you back into position
Removing the ease in your most primary provision
Priming your pumps and resetting your system
Clarifies for you what is from what isn't

Kung Fu master
Exposing the flaws in your technique
Coaxing you to be more Kal-El than Kent
Less oblivious in your intent
More aware of the air in the atmosphere
Prepared for the snares the traps and spears
Because they're there
Disguised to the naked eye
But they appear from time to time
They hurt, they tear, and then subside
Once you find a way to ride the wave
You'll come out on the other side okay

Baby
It's just a hiccup

What Kind of Woman Are You?

What kind of woman are you when no one is watching?
When it's just you and your God
Your dreams and your failures
Your desires and your prayers
When no one else is there

When there is no audience to perform to
When no one can receive your pander
Exchange pleasantries and banter
When you're clear of all the chatter
When you're the only thing that matters

Who decides which lifestyle
Supplies the valuable women
Versus the ones who don't meet the standard?
And why submit to the rules and standards
Forcing us to comply?

Who are they to tell me what is ladylike?
While I do the lady work
Endure how ladies hurt
On a daily basis
We are amazing
Womankind

What kind of goddess style are you rocking?
Six inch stilettos, church shoes and nude stockings
Fresh Air Force Ones, naked toes in the sun
Are you living your life free
Without a concern for anyone's unsolicited opinion?

What kind of lady do you portray to be?
Out here stunting in these streets
Making sure your face is beat
Dressed to the "t"
A dime in a pair of size nines
Too fine to spare time

Are you demure or rowdy?
Meek and passive
Or bold and passionate
Do you argue extra loud
Ostentatious in a crowd
Easily detected
From the way your voice projects
From the back of the room

What kind of woman do they assume you embody?
They address the goddess
But do you treat yourself godly?
They can worship and praise
But do you dance to your heart beat?
Indulge in the masterpiece
Of your unique being
Isn't the sensations weightless and freeing
Untied from the sugar and spice
Living whatever life you like
Released from the banners labeling
Womanhood

No Apologies

Truth be told
I have hurt myself
More than I could ever hurt anyone else
The most damage is done by damaged goods

Damned it

I must manage my womanhood
Before the neighborhood goes to shit
Relay the foundation
The mortar and the bricks on this house
So anything that doesn't fit has to get out

Every room's got to have a use
Each use must be filled with love
Each love must have the best intentions
A fervent mission and tools of precision
To accomplish the goal at hand

The task demands full attention
A watchful eye
Detailed
True to measure

There is no room for error in this project's plan
No recompense for any shortcomings
On this structures uprising
Sharp deadlines and no excuses
For unfinished edges
No corner will be neglected
Built to suit the aesthetic I like
Built to the perspective I have specified
There is nothing in my blue prints about apologizing
For making a way
To be thoroughly delighted and elated
With the makings of me

You So Black

You so black
When you smile the stars come out
When you born the god come out black as night
Dirt
A boot
A hearse
Black to the earth
Black at birth
Black at last
Black at first
Black unrehearsed
Unrequested
Unrequited
Ill invested

Black interested
Black entertained
Black and something special
Baby black just the same
Black like yo mamas and yo daddies
Like you want me but could never have me

Black and inconvenient
With a burden of proof
Until proven innocent
With a built in truth
Black and blue
Black and substance abused
With a life that matters

With hands up don't shoot
With lead in my water
In a sub-par school
Pipelined to prison
Black single mothers with children
Caught up in the system
Tired of the division

Black and broke
Black and poor
Black and bleeding
Black before black was needing social media
Black as Bland
Back to Africa
And black again

Black as ancestors and panthers
Black as Angela and Assata
Black as Betty and Coretta's sons and daughters
Black is pyramids and mathematics
Melanized and magic
Televised and in need of drastic black advancement

Black enhancing black with chances
Black with privilege
With pride
On purpose
On the black hand side
Black and beautiful and blessed
Black and so much more
Nothing less

Black and educated
And dangerous
The most dangerous

Black is brilliant and strong
Black is resilient
Black is song
Hip-hop
Infinite
Black as space
Black has grace
Black has love
Black makes babies
Black babies
Grow up
Black is so tough
Black is so hard to do
Black is me
Black is you

Black is not something you choose
Black is something you charish
Black is something you wear and you rock it with honor
I'm black like my grand-daddy
And my greatest grand-mama
Back to the first farmer of black soil and black seed
Black as you need
Believe
Breathe
Love
Black is all of the above

Always enough
The lift every voice and sing
Letting our freedom ring
And resound

BLACK
Is color, adjective, adverb, and noun
Crown
Clean

To the black as all everlasting
To the black and passing
And every shade of black in between
Matter of fact
Anywhere you believe your black
To at all be applicable
You so black you transcend the physical
Black is original

You so BLACK
You so BLACK
When you smile
The stars come out
You so BLACK
When you born
The god comes out

Sunday Afternoon

Cleaning out my karma's closet
Shaking out the chakra shag rugs from my floor
Sweeping salt out my spirits back door
My soul moves serpentine
Entranced in the charm of the deejay
As he replays my life's soundtrack

Spins back
High school house parties
Kissing in corners
Trading my innocence for an inner sense of womanhood

This moment could go on forever
In the timbre of Smokey's tenor
As the O'Jays okay Sunday dinner
Sunday afternoon is for the sinner
That wasn't up in time for service
While you were in church
Fervently praying for their purpose
And simultaneously complaining to your preacher

You can't control how it moves your soul
When those dusties roll through your speakers
Tension relievers
Back scratchers

Hot lava rock rake massages
Smoothing out the wrinkles in your forehead
The crumpled corners of a soul full of creases
Crevices left from being pressed against the rocks
Crinkled from kicking against the pricks and pushing back
The cardboard container boxing you in
The pine box awaiting your arrival

This music reminds you of living free
Of having love without the needy cling of desperation
It puts you in a place where your memories begin to ease
The troubles you woke up with this morning
Or the one's you let rock you to sleep the night before
You woke up cleaning out your Karma's closet
Shaking out the chakra shag rugs from your floor
Sweeping salt out your spirit's back door
And waiting for the deejay to play
Just one more
Sunday afternoon radio tune
Kitchen cleaning music
Makes you wanna groove with the broom or the vacuum
Spray your Windex while you do a two-step
Tell the deejay
Don't you turn it off yet
The best part is still coming
And my heart is still humming

Family Ties

I came up quick
Like biscuit mix
Instant grits
Grand-mama's shrimp,
Fried in cast iron skillets
Boiling chitterlings
Weaning little ones with pennies and brandy
Pulling out bones that tender gums can't stand
From their bits of catfish
Step up to sit down on big mama's mattress
Kissing her goodnight
Telling her goodbye before the last time she shuts her eyes

I am amassed of Mass's and the will of Wilsons
The heart of Carters and the depth of Wells
Draines and Parkers
Reverends and authors
Unruly daughters, over worked fathers
Mothers who bother very little with bottles of perfume
Children toddle through every room
Except the room where little sister was lost
Swear you get cold soon as you pass the threshold
So some boundaries don't get crossed
Precious life laid at the cross
Born by our family ties
And the cost of time is more valued and less available
As the years go by

And as the years go by
It seems that we are nothing special most times
But together we shine like the diamonds
Clustered on the finger of my mother's hand
Beckoning me home again
Sankofa to the motherland
So close knitted we fitted
To show all the swells and dips of our make up
Take up raising each other's children

Tending open sores and coaxing a healing
From understanding the strength of God
And if you gone cry then go outside
Let your tears water the sod
And let your pain produce fruit too
Let the bittersweet infuse
The meat, the seeds, the juice
Call it your spoonful to help this medicine go down
If you keep your head to the sky
You won't notice the weight of the crown you wear
The worries of the burdens we bear because
We all we got, like it or not

Our collective, however previously neglected
Isn't effective without all our affection
Infecting every broken section
We are reflecting like a corrective mirror
Where blemishes disappear
Because we use proactive loving
It's the salve we rub in
While pulling cornbread from the oven

So sweet that it tastes like cake
Granddaddy couldn't read but studied his word every day
And no, daddy don't have much to say
But his actions impacted and inhabit
Three daughters a father
Can always be proud of

We are the power,
We are God in this hour,
How the Most High defines time
Big mama say we are the future
And the finest prize she'll leave behind
Mama wears her costume broaches
Daddy makes her salmon croquettes
I wrap myself in her patchwork quilt
Breathe deep gather lasting remnants of her scent
Begging for her presence in desperate moments
When my measure of a woman falls short of the mark
When I am alone in the dark I remember I am Clara's heart
Keeper of family secrets and recipes
Passed down like the slant in my eyes when my father smiles
I know the nature of women born wild
I know the sizzle of hot bullets through soft skin
I know the prayers and the psalms that pull breathe back in
When life is leaving
I know the speaking
The interceding
Succeeding when others can't find the answer
I know the off putting sarcasm,
Slick shit talking back water banter
The undeniable southern manner

So ain't no room for fooling,
Ain't but one God for ruling,
And a charge to keep till that great day in the morning

Big Mama said that day is coming,
I wanna tell her that day is here
On this great getting up this morning
I wake up with NO fear
I live with no shame
Wild woman untamed
Mother my first name
Father my foundation
Brick house in the making
Waiting on many mansions
Provision in expansion
Abundance for my family
Amassed of Mass's, Wilsons
Carters, Millenders, Parkers, Draines and Wells'
Our cups, our depths are filled
And we are running over

MASS

MATTER

MAGIC

Could Be

Could be she's plotting on me
She wants to see me in an early grave
Or alone for the rest of my days
Knows the desires of my soul
And uses it to make me her slave
While she makes my misery her mission

I don't think she makes the best decisions
Or has the best intentions
My heart has started my wishing
That the bitch would just stick to ticking and beating
As opposed to leading me to defeated folk
Well practiced in mistreating her and waiting to desert us
She's always loving someone who's trying to hurt us
Or themselves
Or control us
Because they can't control
Themselves

I'm starting to believe the bitch just wants what she sees
As opposed to choosing someone to benefit me
Instead she's a heat seeking missile
Dialed in to locate the bullshit
Fold herself in the falsified feeling
Of a fraudulent lover's embrace

She's brought me boys in men's bodies
Too full of themselves to admit their mistakes
She's brought me criminals, drug dealers,
Murderers, powder heads,
A couple of date rapes

She's brought me cheaters
Ones who say they want you, but don't need you
She's brought me diseased ones
The slap you and then come back
Begging on their knees ones
Closeted gays and brothers fronting to themselves
Because they're too afraid
Or used to fronting for everybody else

Ones who want to marry me
But they've already got wives
Ones that say they love me
While they're having babies on the side
With women they don't even like
The ones who say they love you
But I only see you late at night
And we don't never go outside
Or you can only say I love you
When you're naked and enticed
Buried deep inside

I'm starting to think
My heart doesn't like me very much
I think she's trying to set me up
Hoping I'll break my neck
Falling in love

My heart might be my biggest hater
My most motivated traitor
Benedict Arnold
E Tu, Brute?
Judas, doing her duty
Leading me to my own demise

Now when she speaks I tend to think twice
Because if there is one thing I have learned
About this mound of muscle of mine
Hustling to do more than tick
It's that her track record
When it comes to choosing lovers
Ain't hitting on shit

For Us

If you thought that you were the girlfriend
Until you met his wife
Thought you were wifey,
Till you met the baby mama
If he keeps you on pause like commas
This sanctuary is for you
Because intentions get misconstrued
In the hues of club lights
Weed smoke
Liquor, loneliness and hope
That what you feel
Could not only be real
But last forever

For bottom bitches peeling themselves
From in between the tread wedges of leather boots
And the fibers of doormats
Identities ambiguously hidden under
Codenames in his list of contacts
For those who don't go on many dates in the daylight
But are available at twilight
The wee hours of the morning
Best suited for swing shifts,
White Castle's
Wawa's
And Krystal's

To us re-learning the rules of lady-hood
That our mothers missed
May have forgotten

Or been unavailable to teach
Dutiful, beautiful students
Top of the class
Showing our ass for the master
Mister who kissed her and told her
What fathers' uncles and brothers should have validated
Madams mending mutilated first steps towards self esteem

To the women
Re-establishing personal boundaries
We prisoners of hopeless romanticism
The ones who would do
Damn near anything to be loved
Recovering addicts of attraction
And feigning to be touched
Or just to feel the sensation return after a hearts
Anesthesia has worn off
Waiting to be vulnerable again
Because it's hard work
Pretending you aren't soft
This sacred space is for you
Supreme healers divined and primed
In the pain that desiring love can put you through

The Idea of This Man

I am in love with the idea of this man
I can ponder for hours the power he has over me
If he would only act right
Surrender himself
Fall in line
With my carefully laid plans and designs
I am prone to falling in love with ideas
Concepts, theories, and ambitions
Dreamers love their dreams
Sunrise is a hater
Shedding light on all the half-assed
Plans I drew up in the dark
Sketching my idea of you

Philophobia

I've been Humpty Dumpty posted up on the wall
Been chumped and dumped
Hardly felt the push that caused the fall
Which left me calling for the men who couldn't mend me or
Blend in the cracks in my shell from where I fell
Now the hard head
And soft ass
On this egg
Have split paths

Until our eyes met and attracted me back to old practices
Habits of being posted on your pedestal
Sitting on your wall
Fighting the inevitable,
Knowing I am going to fall

I have fallen for you
Into you
On top of you
Beside you
And around you

And for all this falling I still haven't found you
I have fallen till I finally hit the ground, Boo
Fallen under the weather
Exposed without an umbrella
Only this knitted sweater with my heart stitched on the sleeve
True indeed

I've fallen more like hail than rain
Like mishandled window panes busted into shards
I have fallen hard
Just reunited the fragmented pieces
Where I have fallen apart
Born the scars and contusions
The bangs and the bruises
Don't want to fall in love with stupid
Don't want to fall in love with you
Waiting to hit rock bottom
Waiting for the bottom to fall out
I got too much hind sight for blind faith
Baby, I am all out

But I've fallen for the passion
Fell for the bait and
Ended up trapped in your gaze
Calgon, take me away

When I am with you
Everything falls into place
Falls out of step with the rest of the runners in this rat race
I have fallen
And I can't get up
I may need a back brace made of your embrace
When I've fallen off the wagon
As fools often do
Fallen out of the reach of rescue
And fallen into some deep shit

This is not me attempting to resist
This is just a hope that as we live
We give gravity the fight of its life

Take flight
Take off for a few days
Take off from the runway
Take off all the world's weight
Visit where the sun plays
Kick it where the night stays an hour longer
Than we prayed God would let it
With enough jet fuel and no rules
Me and you could jet set it
From a launch pad in Texas
We could roll it by the pound
Get so high we can't come down
Can't see the ground
Or succumb to that falling feeling
The fall is not at all appealing
Revealing where the ball
And Humpty's heart have been dropped
Plus, falling always leads to
This sudden painful
Stop

So let's not
Fall in love

Let's ball in love
Let's ride in love
Let's hold hands
Partner skate glide in love
Let's pray in love
Cake on the phone late
When one of us is away in love
Let's breathe in love
Be exactly what each other needs in love

Let's try in love
And if we are going to step out on a ledge
Then let's fly in love
Till we end up one hundred years old
Still wrapped up in each other's eyes in love
And die in love

But perhaps
My love
These words are falling on deaf ears
Loving you isn't the issue
My dear
It's the falling that makes me fear
That somewhere along the line
Our line will run out
Or the last grain of sand will have fallen
From the grand hourglass and our time will have run out
And I will have fallen as far from grace as I could fathom
Far from what I imagined
When I managed to fall asleep on my own
Falling into a funk where wishing that you were a love lost
Would have been far better than falling in love alone
So before we both end up falling on our faces
Or making a mistake of what it is we feel
Happening between us can we just
Be grateful we even encountered each other at all
As good as it gets
It still hurts when we slip
Every time
Even I
Fear the fall

Where You Put Me

I have missed you to the bone
Built up your pedestal
Torn down your throne
Left your home feeling the worst kind of alone
Wondering how long before you'd recognize
That I was even gone
Baby was I ever there
Where you say you put me?

They Become

Men
They become
For women never knowing who they were
Before they became
Investment
All my money
All my time
All my fine
Aged like wine
Uncorked and poured
All over the floor
No support
Poured all over the floor
They become a mess
Nobody cleaning but me
No Swiffer sweep
I am on hands and knees
Vinegar and bleach
Elbow grease and sweat
They become flesh
Caught up in the gyration
Caught up in the love making

Imitating their creation of God
Man
Success and sin
Where everybody wins
They become losers, abusers
Heartaches
Headaches
Mistakes
They become the time they take
Full of excuses and uses
Fucked up as he may be
Any day I'd be happy to have him save me
I would gladly have his baby
Creating his son
I ponder
I wonder
What will he become

Diamonds Are Fine

These women bother me very much, attempting to clutch a man's constitution with his fruit or manipulate him with his seed. They call his phone hollering about where they saw him or what they saw him doing. You were six months pregnant the last time you screwed him. Now your baby's turning 2. You're still blue and boohooing.

Boo-boo, I wonder why it doesn't bother you to abuse the bond between a father and his child. There is no disguising it. You lacking the tact to mask the lasting scars of your own father being absent. In all honesty you never wanted any of those circumstances to happen to your own baby. But lately, if he doesn't show up when you like, if he's not all up and through your life, or if he just can't see you as his wife, then you decide to make it hard for him to be involved or do his job.

Content to extend the parental neglect, you're collecting your monthly child support check just like the rest of your "woes is me", absentee baby daddy having homies. You can find them religiously posted up at the currency exchange, pushing double wide strollers down those narrow-ass roped off lanes. You'll end up cashing half of what you used to have when he had it to give of his own free will. Think of how dumb you look, compared to how you must feel.

Your children's father is only trying to rise to an occasion. He requires a little respect, and if so deserved, a standing ovation for doing the job he knows he's supposed to do. He already has the reward he needs from you. You can keep your touching, licking and nookie. Keep your big piece of chicken and cookies.

Madame, obviously you're confused. You must think that the line next to yours on the birth certificate is a place holder for a genetic donor that doesn't have to give a shit. But when he does go beyond and above the call of duty, and everyone around you is well approving of the love and affection he provides his children, you turn from mama to villain. Reportedly your prone to peeling them out of their daddy's arm. All he wants is to be an affectionate father, keep his family from harm and be treated like a man, but you are forcing his hand. There are only so many sides on which this dice can land.

Are you a betting lady? You willing to roll it big? What if the next time you trip or allow foul nomenclature to slip from your lips is the last time he comes to the crib? What if that's the last time he picked up those kids? Whose fault is it then, once the damage has been done, once the rift between child and father has begun to separate such vital ties? Those babies could care less if the two of you are lovers if they can't have their father, their mother and whatever extra loving you can provide. They can't even comprehend the notion of husband and wife. They just need to have their mom and their dad whenever they want or desire.

So why not put how you feel to the side and do what's best for your kids. Get next to the idea of him standing for his. You could have one of these good-for-nothings sitting on their responsibility. Saturate yourself in showering love to these little buds open in innocence and trust. Your gems are robust. They make diamonds of dime pieces and petty thieves with stolen glances dealing fleeting romances.

Give the best you have to this little life God has granted you to care for. Share more of your life with these priceless jewels. You may not be the wife but he values you just as valiantly. Most High divinely entrusted you to raise the family. So don't stress the in-between. Enjoy the blessings you've received. Stop vexing over rings and you'll find that your former pining left you with untold treasures. You'd been holding gold from the mine the whole time. Let your children's brilliance add to your resilience. You got the bling. Look how those babies shine! You may not wear his ring, but trust, his diamonds should do you fine.

Why I Don't Do Cats

Brought a cat in my house
Put a bell around her neck
Cause she stay in my shit
Underfoot
The little bitch stays pawing at my furniture
Scratching up my floor
Stalking the dogs that cross my front porch
The feline is sneaky
Thinking that anytime you leave
The house really belongs to her
The little pussy really pushes me
Spilling her litter wherever she goes
So the ho's got to have a bell
So I can hear every little step
So that even when she thinks she's creeping
She's really telling on herself

Woke Up Broke Up

My sleep is sacred. It is the divine place where my dreams speak to me. I know I can trust the messages, lessons and information imparted in that space. For you, though I am inclined to call truth a lie, altogether denying my connection to the divine.

Spirit always speaks true. She whispers to me about our trysts, that there is bullshit in the midst. And I be like, "Biiiiiiiiiiitch, stop playing. My love is cool. He staying just the way he should. It's all good. Plus, his touch eases just what I need. He makes me sing. He's becoming what I crave." I convince myself that we, I and he, are okay.

These background thoughts though, continue to get in my way. Perhaps it's a prophetic premonition or a touch of clairvoyance. When all I want is to be lost in wanderlust I find it totally annoying. This voice keeps saying we ain't where we used to be. I don't feel like you are still choosing me or our love. Our math is off. We're a fraction of what we was. Something just isn't adding up. Plus, two single units that used to multiply are presently on the divide. Say whatever you like, but I'm beginning to feel like an old Keith Sweat song.

Something, something just ain't right

I doubt you have the desire to confirm or deny any of my suspicions or defend to the otherwise. There is little you can do that I haven't been through with other guys. In the past I ignored the signs and ended up wasting more of both parties' time and energy mending the aftermath of unnecessary melee. I realize this whole scene must seem absolutely crazy. I am learning to listen inward and be quicker to deliver swift justice when spirit requires. Its three a.m. and you must be absolutely tired. But you have to get your things, return your key, put on your coat and shoes. The center of my soul is telling me that I have to stop fucking with you.

To the Sister Who Found Me

To the Sister who found me sleeping with her man,

I must apologize for my behavior.

Now, he never said who you really were, but I was pissing on my women's intuition. I was caught up reminiscing the kiss we'd shared. It wasn't fair to stomp all over your care and I am fucked up for fucking him in the first place.

This will never be okay. And you don't ever have to read or listen to a single word that I write to you or say,

But damn, Sister
I am sorry

For being so sorry
In the first place

Miss Me

He texts me
"I Miss You"
And I am all at once
Flattered and disgusted
Flattered you still think about me
Then disgusted
Recollecting how you ain't about nothing

But I have too much substance
To reply with anything less than polite or negative
So instead he gets
"Thank you for thinking of me and the peace that I bring"
Or
"Peace, King.
Sweet Release, King"
Because I cannot bring myself to say
"I miss you too"
I still remember all the stupid shit you do

Remember?

You already had me
You stashed me
Where I wouldn't interrupt your flow
Where I wouldn't disrupt your stroll
So miss me
While I find a life that feels good to my soul
Miss me
While I become a wife
To someone who understands how I roll

Miss the love you felt when I dealt
And you decided to fold

REMEMBER?

You thought my best wasn't worth your investment
SO MISS ALL OF ME!!
The chef-ing
The late night chill sessions
The shit you told me you couldn't tell anybody else

You really don't miss me anyway

You miss the idea of me
You miss the feeling of me in the air
You miss how when I was around
It seemed like nobody else was there
You miss how I shared my heart
And you thought
Elsewhere the grass would be greener
Or somehow I would become lesser
Or you realized indulging me
Would require some actual effort
And you left my love right where it was

Untouched

Now that your life is too much and your heart is aching
Now that those alternate plans you had in the making
Are coming back to bite you in the ass

Now that it's looking really yellow where you thought
It was going to be greener grass

Now that you are sad
Now that you are afraid
Now
Now you wanna reminisce on old days

Baby
You miss my old ways
The way I used to do things
When I was in love with you
I don't miss what your type of loving do

FOOL, I don't miss you
I don't miss how you make me feel
I don't miss how you sold me lies
On a dream you never intended on making real
I don't miss working so incredibly hard
For the smallest part
Of your empty heart
While you go wherever you are
To do whatever you do
Never checking in on me
Or my state of being
Because you only and ever have room to care about you

I don't miss us
There is no "us" to miss

I don't miss this
False sense of a relationship
That doesn't and never did exist

You miss me
Because you remember my gentleness and my loyalty
I remember how you treated my compassion like a doormat
You miss being able to walk all over me
Like I don't matter

You miss me?
Aww, I'm flattered….and disgusted
I miss you
Like I miss having a whole lot of nothing
Like I miss being the fat girl picked last in gym class
Yeah, like that

I miss you like
Every miserable memory I can muster
Like an abusive lover
That's just what you were
Neglectful and callous
And a stupid ass bastard
Thinking that I like moving backwards
Back to the way you remember things being
"You were always there for me…"
"You always know what to say when shit in my life goes left
field…."
But who's healing my soul
Who's handling me when I am broke
You missed that didn't you
With your missing ass

You missed how I became disgusted with me
For allowing someone like you
To treat me like a second hand citizen

The same one you've been missing since
You stopped feeling the princess you left me
To go find
You're missing your water
But baby, this well is dry
So don't miss me
Please
Miss me
With the bullshit

MASS
MATTER
MAGIC

The Lesson of Loving You

What is required
Is clear
Breathing room

Uninterrupted space

To create a real relationship with letting go
Wanting to be loved is wearing your soul so thin
It's causing your lungs to fold in
You're going to die if you don't expand
Teach yourself how to breathe again
Unlearn your need to need the man
And linger lavishly on the lesson of loving you
With that unconditional God love
With that go out there and make me proud love
With that I know what your tears are about love
With that I'm going to stay right here
Until we figure this shit out love
Subconscious self-love
Like blinking and pumping blood
Like falling down
And getting up

Again

A Mountain

I loved you
As much as I could
As much as God would let me
So it must have been God moving
Telling me
No more, Child
I am trying to save your soul

God has moved me
Before loving
Stole my light
Magic

So... no

There is no thing that I need from you
Nothing that I require
No item I desire
No lost respect or pride
No recuperated tears from my eyes

I am a lover
And these are the crosses
Born in love's loyalty
Though the scars have faded
The memories won't let go of me

God is moving
Saving a lover's soul
I have loved you so much
And my love for you would grow
Far too deeply
To keep loving you
And still truly honor me

And my love deserves honoring
Requires reciprocation
There is no left over time designed for wasting
I cannot stay in
Maintaining
Complaining
Or entertaining this space with you
It's been what it's been, it was what it was
It's cool
If I'm ever cooking food
You are welcome to get a plate
That's the way my love is made

But that old place
We used to operate in
The way we used to be
Is the stuff of memories

God has moved me
And I believe I am a mountain
So for me
Moving on has been a miracle

For CiCi and All My Clients

Section off squares of hair
Relax yourself and the follicles
Where nines lay at the root of your truth
Where wild strands share the rat tails
Of what you've been through
The massage of shampoo across your scalp
Fingertips that snap like
The fairy godmother transforming
The head of Cinderella

No glass slippers for crystals stairs
Deep conditioner to repair
The split of life's necessity
When ends don't meet
Or the means don't justify

To mend the fry of exposure outside
The patches reviving after
Dying to the relentless rain in our existence

Perm the firm
Put the wilds into submission
Or cut the chemical free
Let the chair and the banter
The grease
Seep into your nostrils and breathe

Then speak
The secret only your hair doctor can keep
The advice you've waited two and a half weeks to seek

Planted your booty cheeks in seat
Pumping your rump to a level less stressful
On hands and conversation
Practice perfect patience
Waiting on the sight
Of a better you to come

Better than the one that came in
With the ugly disguise
Baseball caps and shaded eyes
Like you trying to hide from the police
Like a "j" looking for change at the BP

Please be just who you are
So I can invoke the hair gods
To do their job on your coiffeur
Hair disaster absolved
Before you go completely bald
Stressing on the life lessons
The examples you haven't grasped

Holding onto the past
Outdated style
Felt good for a while
Till it took you through messing
Always needed addressing
A dresser full of the product of all you need to maintain
Feeling chained to the vanity
Now you looking for a change
And I am just the one to begin
Your intense cleanse therapy
Treatment,
Regiment,

Supplement,
Supply
It may seem like a lengthy visit
But the hours fly by
With the bootleg dvd, footie sock, and dollar store toy man
Divorce Court or The View or Maury for your enjoyment
As much gossip as you can stand
A moment to forget
A bad ass kid
A cheating man
A fucked up childhood
A foolish mistake
More weight than one living soul should have to take

I offer sanctum
Where the women gather
Thick as blue magic
Beneath my psalms and waving wand
Allies in alloy and Oil of Olay
Steel magnolias forged from Marcel irons
Accentuating your extensions to the Most High
Keep you undeniably fly
Frame the picture of God's immaculate artistry
Construct a crown befitting a queen of your quality
Provide the comfort, courage, confidence you're missing
Translate inner light to outer appearance
You walked in a vision to me
My job is to augment the beauty I already see

Panties, Lipstick, Purse

Change
Daily
For hygiene
For fashion
And the undetermined amount of shit
You are required to carry
To get through your day

MekeTam

Open palmed we are made to play
To the same beat, rhythm and feeling
Celie and Nettie style
In regal fields
Where purple flowers grow wild

Cut from one cloth
Stitched at the hip to the quilt
Made of the pieces we've compiled
Sections of old dresses
Worn in blessings and in messes
In successes and stressing through our failures
In first kissed and tearful farewells
I will ever be wrapped in your spell

And if the stars ever fell from the sky
I could still count the stars in your eyes
Sparkling in their corners
Our love is so much stronger than the bindings of time
So much longer than the mind could define

Something like divine
Like turning water into wine
Like turning whining into late night chatter and laughter
Like me going out first and you following after only
Much, much faster
The memories make me
Wish we could go back to
When we first fashioned mud-cake recipes
When I cried hard

Good Lawd
When mama started whooping y'all
Till she ended up whooping me
When your little bad asses learned to read
Breaking into my diary
Realizing my life was inspiring to someone so special
The only ones I could stand next to
And know without asking you'd always have my back
And be by my side
You are a sister's pride

Sensing the silliness of men
When I had no sense in choosing them
Taking my mistakes and using them to your advantage
Doing so much better than you'd seen
Best believe
I learned to weave, braid and cut hair
So you would appear
Much flyer than I did in my high school yearbook pics

We talk shop and talk shit
Sweet Shug Avery with grit
That sticks to ribs and slides off walls
We clean up each other's messes
Catch each other
Trust fall

Trust fall to come although autumn alters out regal fields
And we harvest the yield
Until the winter white wipes us clean again
Until we can play like it's spring again
And sing again

Me and you
Us never part

Me and you
Us be the light inside the stars
Me and you
Us be the spark that jump starts hearts
I'll be with you no matter where you are
If God should ever make us part
You will never be far from my soul
From my thoughts

You are the reason I write poetry and go to these open mics
Hoping life will open up a doorway
To some young black queen
In need of a sister's advice and guidance
Like...

Be a lion in your fire
Defiant
Reliant
Though the times be trying
Trying their best to keep you from besting your test
Trying their best to keep you and your best from manifesting
Trying their best to keep you from becoming
The woman that you are meant to be

I write selfishly to my sisters for my sisters
With the admittance that I have been and played the victim
But this isn't written to wallow with them
This is conviction
Call it divination
Incantation of protection

On your right
On your left
When you step
When you take a breath
When you are too afraid to pray for yourself
I will be there to say your Hail Mary's and your ase's

If I may intercede on behalf of my sisters
God is listening
His eye is on the sparrow
Sister, I am keeping my eye on you
I feel you so deep in my marrow
That I bleed when you get wounded
So I sing you through your bruises with my blues
Till we be baptized in his blood
Where the red and blue infuse
And we are open purple buds
Planted in love
With pedals that touch
And leaves that clap hands
Sense to bend in the wind
To rise after giving in

Like wildflowers
Like women
Like the oceans and seas we swim in
Could never pull us asunder
You
Wonderment of woman
Reflection of my mama
Perfect peace
A piece of me
And nothing but death could keep me from you

No substance could subdue
My hope for you to know
That you are truly something too
So shake your shimmy
Till you hear me clear enough
I am your
S-I-S-T-E-R
Period

Naked

There are scars
Tender bruises
Blacks, blues and
Sensitive tissues
I have issues

There is damage
They have managed
To leave marks

I am lucky
All the scars lay in this broken heart
There are no broken bones
No contusions
Just confusion

How could you do it?
And how could I let it get done?
Why did I run to you?
Why didn't I have the sense to run?
Could this be the worst thing
I've run to?
Or that I've run from?

They are sons
They are not guns
But they are weapons of mass distractions
I carry the consequences of their actions

Good girls go bad
Good women go worse
Go harder
Go farther
Carry the hurt longer
Burden the brunt of the baggage better
Forget to remember how to the weather of the storm

Next time the opportunity comes
I will be more transparent

Naked

My scars will be exposed
I will point to each one and bare my soul
I will show him where his scar will go
Because I know he won't mean to
I know he won't seem to
But he will lean too hard on one of my fragile points
And knock my whole structure off its joints

I will not mean to mistrust him
He will not mean my destruction
Neither intent will keep eruptions
From making their way to the surface
He will mean well in his service
Even stick around for the after quakes

Maybe he will have what it takes
Maybe we will have our mistakes and our successes
Maybe we will be each other's last next if
We meet one another
Naked

Slow Cooker

All day simmering
Beans soaked, sifted
Peaches peeled, pitted
And set aside

Alive
On time
Like Jesus
Main line
Sound to the deaf
Sight to the blind
Bread for the begging
And dough for the poor

You feel like every open door
Perfect breezes in unbearable heat
Cool sand underneath my feet
Every one of my favorite treats
No calories
A compliment to me
No flattery
A hard act to beat
No battery
But definitely in charge
A god

We are not ordinary people
But maybe if we do take it slow
Perhaps we can grow

A hybrid human spirit
God body love
Unlike anybody else's
Something just for us

I just want a friend
To fuck
And do weird shit with
To save my money and build with
Someone to hug
While we watch Netflix or PornHub
Someone to love
Who'll clean out the bathtub every once in a while
Somebody that makes me smile
And laughs at my jokes
Thinks I'm the most
Even when I'm at my least

All this kinging and queening
With folks fronting
Like they know the meaning
I used to be one of the ones fronting too
Passionate and dogmatic in my youth
Now I'm just too old and I don't need anymore
Hotep whoring bro's
Third eye preachers,
Kemetic method master teachers,
Seven chakra soul rockers.
Metaphorical metaphysical meditations,
Alkaline alchemic vibration
Ascension pretenders
I'm trying to keep it simple

I'm content with
Some good ole regular love
The kind that don't require much
A meal and some roll up
A bottle and sure enough
Us
Up
Turnt
Lit
Drunk as shit and kicking it
Like friends
Who also get to fuck

Slow
Steady
Prepared to marinate
Till everything comes
Together

Even Before

Takes all of my patience
Makes me wait
But always picks me up when I ask him to

Eats all my food
May not always go to church
But searches for my Easter dinner
Lingers for my leftovers

Writes me poetry
Sweats for me
Makes other women flirt
I love to watch him work
I like to watch them want what I got
No claim on
He flame on
Came home on his own accord

My best friend
We make amends
And make mistakes
We make each other great
Hurt when the other has to go away
Stay as long as we can
Standing even when the sands sink beneath us

He's
A builder
Child of God
A man with a plan

Reminds me of my dad
Takes care of business
By hook or by crook
Does the best he can by me
And never says what he cannot do
Lets me kiss away his blues
Some times
Most times
Neither one of us knows just what to do
Or how to move
Or how to prove ourselves
Worthy to use the tools we've been given

Under less preferential conditions
Our collision could be tragic but
Our love is different and magic
And has the advantage of knowing
All the ways it could go wrong
But we are bonded strong

I fuck with him the long way
We make God shout on Sundays
Graced with a gift only God could make
A love no living soul could take
No one can emulate his particular technique
The way he smells
The way he breathes
The way he speaks
Even his bullshit sounds sweet
That look in his eye makes me weak
He sees my triggers and he treats this loaded gun with care

Aware and prepared
Even when he's scared
My automatic reaction
Is protecting his back
Right by his side
I'm there
Even when I'm not
He got my prayers
Even when he's not aware of the intercession
He's a blessing
And my hearts curse
No one could love me better
No one could hurt me worse
I Proverbs 31
He ended his search

We work
We fit
We fight
We kiss
Make up
Make love

We make love do what it does
Even when it doesn't
We got something of substance
Because he knew who he was
Even before
When he wasn't

Fragile and Free

I don't want to change you
Rather take you just the way you are
Every single part
Especially your heart
If you will let me have it
I will treat it like glass
You are fragile and free
You rest next to this vessel and you see the same thing

We
Kingdom
Me
Queendom
Goddess
Mermaid
Magic

We are nothing like the others
We are good choices and bad habits
We are addicts of the loving
We recover with each other
We are nothing like the others
He is not another brother
He is not your average nigga
He is thought process configured into god body
Considerate of himself and everyone else
Especially me

He considers me
My heart
The parts I keep in the darkest places
I can find to hide
He considers it a pleasure to endeavor
To even try
He considers me fly
He considers us right
He considers a life with him by my side
That's why he is here
And he gets it
Oh, he gets it
He lets it hold him captive
He keeps me captivated

We are giving
We are taking
Advantage of the chance
We've been living
We've been patient
Endured the circumstances
Enhanced ourselves in waiting
And made ourselves prepared
For whatever lies ahead

Now I've been lonely and I've been scared
Fighting to keep the playing field fair
And my attitude no worse for the wear
And I am all too aware it's been wearing me out
Working my nerves
Keeping me curbed
So I don't go serving no bitter bites and calling it delight

I am sweet tea
Nectar of the gods
Quenching his appetite
He won't fight what's coming in the might of this woman

I am something I love
So it's easy being something he love
We are all of the above
When one answer is not enough to cover the subject
I am subject matter he adores to flatter
I am outer stratosphere
He is the atom
I am the atmosphere
We are a universe
And everything that happens here
Is life
And miracles
We are a universe of miracles
And who would change a miracle

I want you just the way you are
We are brilliant stars
Summing up our parts
Especially our hearts

Fragile and free

Morning Ritual

We sort out our parts
Pull the you from me
The we
From sleep
Figure out whose
Hands, breath and feet
Belong to each

Before there is movement
We share meditation and libation
Smoke curling underneath our dreams
Everything swirling towards the sky
Including you and I

Taste the melanin
Rising thick from our throats
Creeping vines
Sun salutation seedlings
Breaking through to the daylight

We are heart beats and smiles
Pheromones and priorities
Tussling sheets
Extra taps to the snooze button

This

This is the best part of waking up.

A Love Poem

We play
We talk
We eat
We sleep
We breathe
We breathe deep
We hold
We release

We constructors of speech
Convicted but free
We lips
Tongue
We teeth
We tactile
We reach
We the scriptures that teach
The collective
While each
Each other's lover blood
Floods we bleed
Until we drown in this sea

We love we lovely
We love we hugging
We love it tugging
At heart strings plucking
Our love note tucking in envelope
Licking closed
Hopeful perfect in passing

Admirer ripping open
Time stops
We are elapsing
We are stars crossed
Time travelling universes
Unrehearsed

This is improvisation
And we make it what we want it to be
Like on stages
Like in prayers
Like in my dreams
Manifested to my destiny
Sealed to my desires
Motivations for this artist to aspire

We water
We fire
We title bout fighters
So pretty
So pretty we flyer than butterflies or bees
Than the tops of redwood trees
Than skyscrapers tearing holes in the clouds
When the rain comes down we dance in it
Splash and ruin our best pants in it
Because we are washer and dryer
Sativa and lighter
Mike and Ikes
Now and Laters
Good and Plenty
Like Forrest and Jenny
Baby we are peas and carrots

We inherit the best our parent could show
We grow
We are like Lisa and Hakeem
You know what that means?
We let our Soul Glow
We are solos
We are two roads laid parallel
Getting there one step at a time
We are rhythm and rhyme
Blues and blue lines
Ink and computer keys

We are you and me
Doing the damn thing
No sampling
We empty mpc's
We are emcees
Mp3-ed
We are die hard
IPod
Video tripods
Viewed on YouTube
Weaving a voodoo
We Shango
We Osun
We middle passage travelling through oceans
We the ingredients to this love potion
Bubbling in this cauldron
We smoldering
We scalding
We forty fives revolving
With no scratches and no skips

Look baby
No scratches
No skips
It's like magic still exists

We touch
We kiss
We embrace and
It's bliss
And we love it
Like this

Affirmation

I am well
You are well
We are our best selves
Self is all we really have
I pray that you are happy
And if you are sad
I pray the sadness teaches
What it must and moves along

Stay strong
In connection
In convictions
In vivid vision
Outside the system
Above the fog
Head to the sky
Skin in the sun
Blue as the night
Black as they come

We are the ones
Making things better
Together
Enjoy the weather
Whether weather withers, wains or warms
Through the eye of the hurricane
Till it subsides to the storm

I pray that today you are okay
With every decision you make
Whichever turn your life may take
I pray that I be okay with it
Universally submitted
Because I can only control my decisions

We have been given
Millions of provisions
Valuable talents
It's our task to grab them
And tactfully have them
Work to our benefit
One to another
Beneficial
Work collectively
Through our issues
And handle the rest like it ain't no sweat
We are the best individuals I have met

I can only pray for we
For you and me
That I be phenomenal
All by myself
That you be phenomenal
All by yourself
That we be phenomenal
When we are together

That we be greater than the sum of our parts
That we be stronger than our base desires
That we aspire and attain higher
That I love better than I have in previous practice
That every time we connect we make practice a habit
Elevated and grounding
The you around me
The love around we
The purpose in front of each
You
And
I
We live in love
On purpose
In service
I pray
I give it all away
In good faith
With honest intention
And space
Selah
Asé

Made in the
USA
Columbia, SC